Sauropods

Giant Plant-Eating Dinosaurs

by Grace Hansen

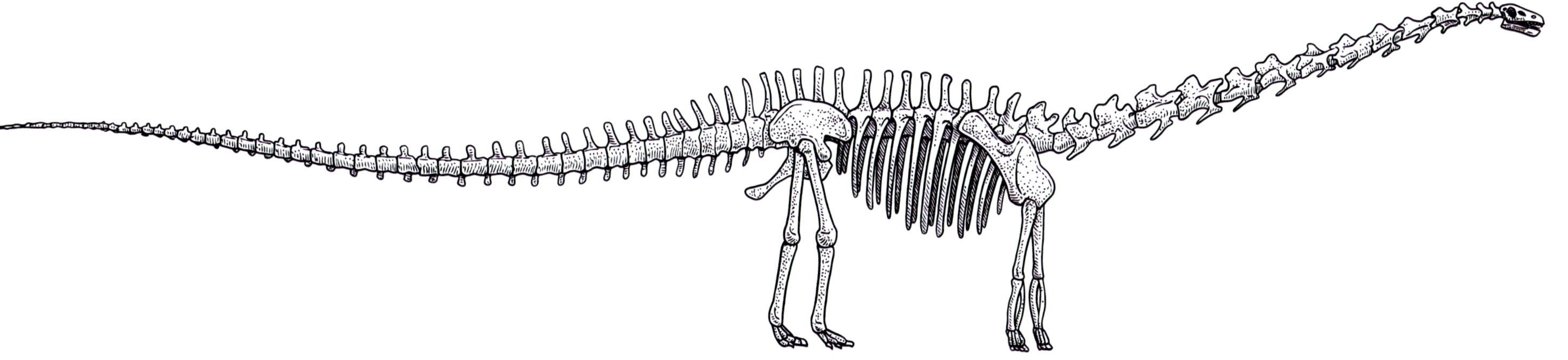

Abdo Kids Jumbo is an Imprint of Abdo Kids
abdobooks.com

abdobooks.com

Published by Abdo Kids, a division of ABDO, P.O. Box 398166, Minneapolis, Minnesota 55439.

Printed in the United States of America, North Mankato, Minnesota.

052025

092025

Photo Credits: Adobe Stock, Alamy, Getty Images, Science Source, Shutterstock

Production Contributors: Teddy Borth, Jennie Forsberg, Grace Hansen
Design Contributors: Victoria Bates, Candice Keimig

Library of Congress Control Number: 2024947619

Publisher's Cataloging-in-Publication Data

Names: Hansen, Grace, author.

Title: Sauropods: giant plant-eating dinosaurs / by Grace Hansen

Other Title: giant plant-eating dinosaurs

Description: Minneapolis, Minnesota : Abdo Kids, 2026 | Series: Dinosaur groups | Includes online resources and index.

Identifiers: ISBN 9798384905172 (lib. bdg.) | ISBN 9798384905875 (ebook) | ISBN 9798384906223 (read-to-me ebook)

Subjects: LCSH: Dinosaurs--Juvenile literature. | Prehistoric animals--Juvenile literature. | Animals, Fossil--Juvenile literature. | Paleontology--Juvenile literature.

Classification: DDC 567.90--dc23

Table of Contents

The Giant Plant-Eating Dinosaurs

Sauropods were a group of dinosaurs. They lived from the Early Jurassic into the Cretaceous Period. They were found throughout the world.

Jurassic

201 million years ago

Cretaceous

145 million years ago

Sauropods

Sauropods were the biggest animals to ever walk the Earth. The smallest members of the group could grow up to 50 feet (15 m) long. The largest members could grow up to 80 feet (24 m)!

Sauropods are known for their very long neck and tail. Their neck could reach food high in trees. Their tail was powerful. It may have been used to fight off **predators**.

Because of their size, sauropods lived in open areas. They likely preferred warm, wet **climates**. Plants could grow all year long in these places.

Sauropods were **herbivores**. They had peg-like teeth to help pluck leaves from plants. They had to eat a lot of food each day to fill their giant stomachs!

Spinophorosaurus

The discovered remains of *Spinophorosaurus* are some of the most complete of any early sauropod. Its name comes from the two pairs of large spikes near the end of its tail.

Middle Jurassic
Fossils found in
Africa
As long as
half a tennis court
40 ft (12 m) long
As heavy as an
African elephant
15,000 lbs
(6,800 kg)
Spinophorosaurus

Apatosaurus

Apatosaurus was very big. It likely had to eat up to 1,000 pounds (454 kg) of food each day! *Apatosaurus* lived in **herds**. This protected them from **predators**.

Apatosaurus
Late Jurassic
Fossils found in
North America
As long as
2 school buses
70 ft (21 m) long
As heavy as a
full concrete truck
70,000 lbs
(31,750 kg)

Diplodocus

Diplodocus lived among *Apatosaurus*. They did not weigh as much as *Apatosaurus* but would have been longer. This was due to their very long tail.

Late Jurassic
Fossils found in
North America
As long as a
baseball base line
90 ft (27 m) long
As heavy as a
coach bus
33,000 lbs
(15,000 kg)
Diplodocus

Dreadnoughtus

Dreadnoughtus was the largest land animal that ever lived. Its neck made up about 37 feet (11 m) of its length. It could reach leaves high up in trees.

Dreadnoughtus
Late Cretaceous
Fossils found in
South America
As long as a
blue whale
85 ft (26 m) long
As heavy as
9 African Elephants
100,000 lbs
(45,300 kg)

Common Sauropod Features

Glossary

climate – the usual weather conditions in a place.

herbivore – an animal that only feeds on plants.

herd – a group of wild animals that feed and travel together.

predator – an animal that hunts other animals for food.

Index

Visit **abdokids.com** to access crafts, games, videos, and more!

Use Abdo Kids code

DSK5172

or scan this QR code!